INDOOR WILDLIFE

Revealing the Creatures Inside Your Home

INDOOR WILDLIFE

Revealing the Creatures Inside Your Home

GERARD E CHESHIRE

WHITE OWL
AN IMPRINT OF PEN & SWORD BOOKS LTD.
YORKSHIRE – PHILADELPHIA

First published in Great Britain in 2019 by
Pen and Sword White Owl
An imprint of
Pen & Sword Books Ltd
Yorkshire - Philadelphia

Hardback ISBN: 978 1 52672 973 6
Paperback ISBN: 978 1 52675 174 4

Typeset in Cormorant By Mac Style

Printed and bound in India by Replika Press Pvt. Ltd.

Pen & Sword Books Ltd incorporates the Imprints of Pen & Sword Books
Archaeology, Atlas, Aviation, Battleground, Discovery, Family History, History,
Maritime, Military, Naval, Politics, Railways, Select, Transport, True Crime, Fiction,
Frontline Books, Leo Cooper, Praetorian Press, Seaforth Publishing, Wharncliffe and
White Owl.

For a complete list of Pen & Sword titles please contact

PEN & SWORD BOOKS LIMITED
47 Church Street, Barnsley, South Yorkshire, S70 2AS, England
E-mail: enquiries@pen-and-sword.co.uk
Website: www.pen-and-sword.co.uk

or

PEN AND SWORD BOOKS
1950 Lawrence Rd, Havertown, PA 19083, USA
E-mail: Uspen-and-sword@casematepublishers.com
Website: www.penandswordbooks.com

CONTENTS

INTRODUCTION

This book examines the environments inside our homes that offer sanctuary and somewhere to live for many animals and a few plants. In essence, these are species that naturally take up residence in caves, cliffs, tree cavities, nests, burrows and so on. They therefore find our homes suitable for habitation because they offer similar microhabitats. Some species flourish in dry dark places, while others prefer damp dark places.

The term 'synanthropic' is used to describe species that live alongside humans. Those that actually live on our bodies, or else feed on our blood, are known as parasites. As a rule, all synanthropic animals and plants benefit in one way or another from their association with humans, but we do not, unless we consider the educational value of studying them. A few species can be harmful to our health and wellbeing, but most are just benign companions.

The best way to examine synanthropic species is to think of our homes as collections of different habitats that different species find attractive for different reasons.

Beneath our houses we have voids, undercrofts, basements and cellars, which all offer habitats similar to caves and underground cavities. In addition, sheds, outhouses, garages and summerhouses offer similar habitats, where animals can shelter from the elements and where lighting and heating are generally absent.

Inside our houses, we have a variety of rooms, each offering different facilities to wildlife. Living rooms and bedrooms have furniture and carpets. Bathrooms have water and moist air. Kitchens have supplies of foodstuffs. All offer warmth in the winter and coolness in the summer.

Above our houses we have roofs, attic spaces, lofts, chimneys and eaves, which offer shelter from the elements and protection from predators. And on the outside of our houses we have walls, which offer cavities and surfaces that are useful to certain species.

All-in-all then, our homes offer a wide range of habitats to the many species that might be classed as synanthropic. If we include offices, farms, churches, shops, restaurants, municipal buildings, factories and so on, then clearly there are many more environments available to species that are able to exploit them.

MAMMALS

FOXES

The red fox has adapted very well to living alongside humans. Of course, foxes have always been troublesome to rural communities and farms, due to their habit of preying on small livestock, such as poultry, rabbits and lambs. Indeed, that is why there used to be a tradition of fox hunting throughout Britain. Curiously, fox hunting is inordinately expensive per fox culled, when one considers the cost of keeping hounds, stabling horses and kitting riders in their fancy attire, not to mention the time and effort involved. It therefore makes far better sense to pay for the services of marksmen and trappers, who are far more efficient and humane in their approach to culling the animals.

These days, foxes have become far more abundant in urban environments, because they have plenty of buildings beneath which to make their lairs, and an abundance of food, either scavenged or offered to them. As a result, many people, in town and country, witness foxes in their gardens and living beneath their homes or out buildings. Although one occasionally hears about foxes displaying aggression towards humans, it is usually reserved for cats and dogs, which present a far greater threat to them.

RODENTS

BROWN RAT AND HOUSE MOUSE

Brown rats and house mice are the scourge of many householders in Britain. Both species are very good at exploiting human habitations and foodstuffs. They are able to gnaw their way into properties and into food containers. They also gnaw a wide variety of materials into bedding for making their nests. As a result, rats and mice can become established very quickly and multiply very rapidly too.

The main issue with the presence of rats and mice is hygiene. As they leave their droppings and urine on floors and surfaces, then germs are spread through the indoor environment. They also contaminate anything they touch with germs, so that people can easily become ill and diseased. In addition, rats and mice carry fleas, which transfer to domestic animals and humans. Bubonic plague, sometimes known as the black death, was famously spread across Europe by rodents carrying fleas.

Although rats and mice are to be admired for their adaptability and versatility, it is best to keep them out of our homes. As well as ridding a house of the rodents and blocking points of entry, it is a good idea to keep foodstuff stored in such a way that rodents cannot access them. Also, think about bins, compost heaps and bird feeders, as they are all restaurants for vermin. If they have no food, then they will move elsewhere.

Brown rat: The brown rat is a versatile and ubiquitous pest, in urban, suburban and rural places. *Rattus norvegicus.* (Steve Herring)

House mouse: The house mouse is associated with houses because it is so good at finding its way through tiny spaces into our homes. *Mus musculus.* (Rascal Tinian)

DORMOUSE

The edible dormouse will often use roof-spaces of houses for nesting. The animals don't present a problem like rats and mice, as they feed outside, but they will gnaw materials to make their nests and can be quite noisy. Also, their droppings can accumulate, so it is probably wise to discourage them by blocking points of entry. Of course, one might also install nest boxes in one's garden, so that the dormice have alternative accommodation when they have been evicted. Dormice also hibernate during the uncongenial months, so they need somewhere dry and secure in order to survive the winter.

Edible Dormouse: The edible dormouse has its name because 'dor' is a European Medieval word for sleep, due to its hibernation in winter. *Glis glis.* (Peter Dean)

BATS

Although bats deposit droppings and urine beneath their roosts, most people consider it a privilege to have bats living in their roof spaces or behind their shutters. As a result, they often accommodate bat toiletry habits by placing trays below the bats in order to catch their excreta and periodically remove it.

There is something special about having bats in one's house, almost like a badge of honour. Perhaps this is because their presence is indicative of an environment that is healthy enough to feed them. Also, they have a mysterious quality and do not present a hazard to humans. Whatever the reason, bats benefit from this tolerance and acceptance greatly, in villages, towns and cities throughout Britain.

Bats are also protected by law, in Britain, giving them an additional cachet. Although some species are very common, the protection extends to all species because bats often live in mixed colonies and different species can also be quite tricky to identify and separate from one another.

Some bats like to hang freely from their roost, such as horseshoe bats, but most prefer to crawl between vertical surfaces, where they feel safe from predators. As a result, it isn't always evident that bats are present without further investigation. The commonest British bats found in houses are the pipistrelles, of which there are two species: the common pipistrelle *Pipistrellus pipistrellus* and the soprano pipistrelle *Pipistrellus pygmaeus*. Both species are very small and can fit through spaces as tight as 15mm x 20mm. This means that they can roost under tiles, behind soffit boards, between walls and beams and so on. They feed on small flying insects at dusk and at night.

Common Pipistrelle: The common pipistrelle bat is one of the commonest species to frequent houses, as it is small and able to squeeze through tight apertures. *Pipistrellus pipistrellus*. (Olivier Bxl)

Soprano Pipistrelle:
The soprano pipistrelle
bat has a higher pitch
to its calls, because it
is slightly smaller than
the common pipistrelle.
Pipistrellus pygmaeus.

BIRDS

A number of bird species will utilize buildings for making their nests and rearing their young. House sparrows and starlings are well known for nesting between the eaves of houses. They find points of access and build their nests on top of the house walls, so that they are protected from the weather and from predators.

Jackdaws and gulls like to build their nests on chimneystacks. Gulls need the relatively flat surfaces between the chimney pots, but jackdaws will nest inside the chimney. They wedge sticks across the flue until they have made a secure platform and then build the nest on top.

House martins are able to build their nests hanging below the overhang of roofs, because they use mud, which sticks to the two surfaces and then dries hard. Swallows also use mud, but they build their nests on top of beams, where there is more support.

Robins and blackbirds will sometimes nest in curious places within buildings. Often it is because they cannot find suitable locations in gardens, either because there are none available or because they have already been taken. So they search for places in sheds and outhouses.

The great tit and blue tit quite often nest in wall cavities, as long as the opening is sufficiently small to prevent predators from reaching their eggs or chicks. Town pigeons also utilize wall apertures, although they need to be much larger.

House Sparrow: The house sparrow has lived in association with people for thousands of years, as we have provided it with accommodation and food. *Passer domesticus.*

Starling: The starling is sometimes confused with the blackbird, but it has a shorter tail and speckled plumage. *Sturnus vulgaris.* (C. Feet)

House Martin: The house martin has a distinctive white rump, which is clearly seen when the bird is in flight. *Delichom urbicum.*

Barn Swallow: The barn swallow often uses old windows and doorways to access nesting places in outbuildings. *Hirundo rustica.* (Asa Berndtsson)

Blackbird: The female blackbird has brown plumage for camouflage whilst sitting on the nest. *Turdus merula.* (Brian Snelson)

Great Tit & Blue Tit: The great tit and blue tit are small enough to make the most of crevices between wall stones. *Parus major. Cyanistes caeruleus.* (P. Paul)

(Nick Ford)

Robin: The robin will often nest on shelves and ledges inside outbuildings if there is a suitable opening for entry and egress. *Erithacus rubecula.* (Bill Hails)

Town Pigeon: The town pigeon is descended from the rock dove, which naturally nests on cliff ledges. *Columbia livia.* (Phillip Goddard)

Jackdaw: The word 'daw' is the old English name for this bird, whilst the word 'jack' imitates its call, so we have jack-daw. *Corvus monedula.* (Asa Berndtsson)

Herring Gull: The herring gull, and the similar lesser black-backed gull, will often nest on rooftops many miles from the coast. *Larus argentatus.* (John Haslam)

INVERTEBRATES

By far the majority of animal species that invade our homes are invertebrates. This is largely because they are small enough to gain entry through cracks around doors and windows, or to simply enter unnoticed when doors and windows are open. Others hitch rides on our pets or on our clothing and hair.

SPIDERS

The invertebrates that people notice the most are house spiders, because they grow to such a large size and wander about, looking for mates. Many people are fearful of spiders. This seems to be an instinctive reaction, probably because it was wise to avoid potentially harmful spiders when early humans inhabited caves and rock shelters, so the behaviour became innate.

Barn Spider: The barn spider has proportionately long legs, making it look rather more fearsome than the house spider. *Eratigena atrica*. (G. Cheshire)

House Spider: The house spider is often encountered wandering about the house, on walls ceilings and floors. *Tegenaria domestica.* (Cristophe Quintin)

Daddy Longlegs: The daddy longlegs has such long legs so that it can span the gaps in its random web. *Pholcus phalangioides.* (Sam Snook)

False-widow: The false-widow tends to secrete itself in dark places, such as within cupboards or under furniture. *Steatoda nobilis*. (David Short)

House spiders have been known to bite humans on the odd occasion. Their venom is not toxic to humans, but it can lead to secondary infections and necrosis where the venom kills the cells around the bite, so it is always best to avoid contact with house spiders when one's skin is thin enough to bite. The skin on one's hands is too thick to bite through, but they will have a go if they feel threatened.

There are various similar looking species known as house spiders. The giant house spider, or barn spider *Eratigena atrica* is the largest. Other smaller species belong to the genus *Tegenaria*, such as the common house spider *Tegenaria domestica*. House spiders are known as funnel web spiders, because they make a funnel shaped web for catching their prey, usually in a corner where insects are likely to wander.

Zebra Spider: The zebra spider is an expert at stalking and pouncing on prey, rather like a miniature tabby cat. *Salticus scenicus.* (Nick Goodrum)

Pink Velvet Spider: The pink velvet spider uses the cover of darkness to catch prey insects while they are dormant. *Clubiona terrestris.* (G. Cheshire)

There are various other species of spider commonly found in British houses. The daddy longlegs spider *Pholcus phalangioides*, sometimes known as the cellar spider, is familiar to many. It constructs a random web in dark corners in order to ensnare small flying insects. The spider is quite small with proportionately long legs and has a distinctive habit of shaking its web when disturbed.

A recent newcomer to many British homes is the false-widow spider *Steatoda nobilis*, so called because it has a similar shape to the infamous black widow spider. Its bite is similar to a red ant sting for most people, but a few people have been known to suffer anaphylactic shock, which is an extreme allergic reaction to the venom.

The zebra spider *Salticus scenicus* is a small jumping spider that usually lives on the external roofs and wall of houses, but it will occasionally come inside

Bulbous Harvestman: The bulbous harvestman has a rounded bulb-like body shape and is reddish-brown in colour. Harvestmen have the ability to deliberately lose a leg when distressed. This is a defence against predators, as the leg keeps moving rapidly as a distraction whilst the harvestman makes its getaway. It is called autotomy and explains why harvestmen often have fewer than eight legs. *Leiobunum rotundum.* (N. Mahieu)

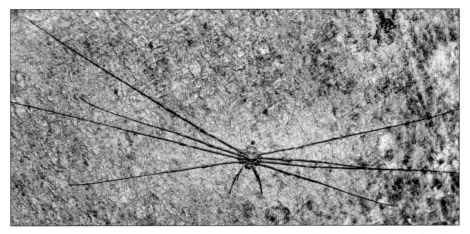

Branching Harvestman: The branching harvestman has antler-like pedipalps, which is uses to hold items of food. *Dicranopalpus ramosus*. (Mick Talbot)

to hunt. It does so by stalking small insects, such as fruit flies, ants and aphids, and then leaping onto them.

The pink velvet spider *Clubiona terrestris* is a harmless medium sized sac spider that often comes into homes. It walks relatively slowly at night, in search of insects at rest on walls and ceilings, which are easy prey. During the day it hides in a nook or cranny where it builds a resting sac from silk.

In addition to spiders, there are other arachnids in and around our houses. Harvestmen or Opiliones, are similar to spiders, but they have just one body part instead of two, and their legs are relatively long and thin. Harvestman

Basket Harvestman: The basket harvestman has a low-slung body, so that its legs create a basket-like arrangement. *Opilio canestrinii*. (Martin Cooper)

have their name because they are most abundant in late summer, when crops are ready to harvest. Spiders are hunters of live prey, but harvestmen are omnivorous scavengers, often eating dead animal matter. They are sometimes found resting on walls during the day, where they flatten themselves by stretching out their legs. At night they wander about looking for food and use their legs to lower themselves down like miniature cranes. There are about 25 species of harvestman in Britain. Some typical examples are bulbous harvestman *Leiobunum rotundum*, the branching harvestman *Dicranopalpus ramosus,* and the basket harvestman *Opilio canestrinii.*

The other arachnids found in our homes are far smaller than spiders and harvestmen. They include book scorpions, mites and ticks. Book scorpions *Chelifer cancroides*, or house false scorpions, are tiny arachnids with scorpion-like claws that prey on dust mites *Dermatophagoides pteronyssinus* and book lice

Book Scorpion: The tiny book scorpion uses its clawed pedipalps to catch and then hold its prey while it eats it alive. *Chelifer cancroides.* (Laa Jala)

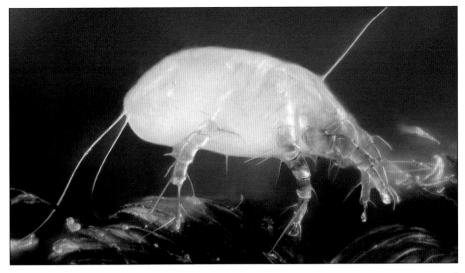

Dust Mite: The dust mate is almost invisible to the human eye, so it goes unnoticed living in our carpets and rugs. *Dermatophagoides pteronyssinus.* (Giles San Martin)

Trogium pulsatorium & *Liposcelis bostrychophila,* which are microscopic insects, often colloquially known as bookworms. They also prey on the larvae of small moths, beetles and flies. Book scorpions hitch rides on adult insects in order to relocate themselves in search of food and mates.

Velvet mites, or wall mites *Eutrombidium rostratus, Balaustium murorum* & *Trombidium holosericeum* are bright red arachnids often found swarming over

Beaked Velvet Mite: The beaked velvet mite has unusually long and curved forelegs and pedipalps. *Eutrombidium rostratus.* (Lukas Litz Obb)

Wall Velvet Mite: The wall velvet mite has a relatively small body and long legs for running about on hard surfaces. *Balaustium murorum.*

Silky Velvet Mite – adult: The silky velvet mite has a velour-like texture to its plump body. *Trombidium holosericeum.* (Chris Fifield)

Silky Velvet Mite – nymphs: The nymphs of silky velvet mites are parasites of harvestmen and other invertebrates. *Trombidium holosericeum.* (G. Bohne)

walls and paving. They do so in order to breed, as the males deposit sperm packets on the surface, which the females then collect. As larvae, these mites are parasites of other arthropods, including harvestmen.

The majority of people are unknowingly playing host to face mites, which are microscopic arachnids. The adult mites are less than 0.5mm in length and translucent. Face mites *Demodex folliculorum* lives in the hair follicles on peoples' faces, while gland mites *Demodex brevis* lives in the sebaceous glands,

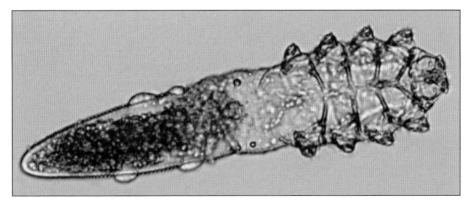

Face Mite: The face mite is slender in shape, so that it can live inside hair follicles. *Demodex folliculorum.* (K.V. Santoch)

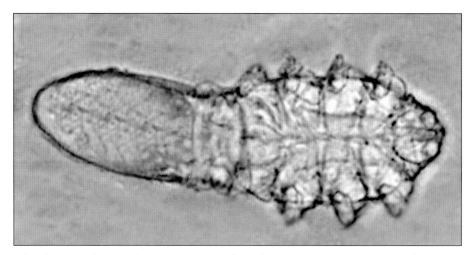

Gland Mite: The gland mite is shorter than the face mite, as it lives inside the oil glands in the skin. *Demodex brevis.* (K.V. Santoch)

which produce the protective oil on our facial skin. For the most part Demodex mites are harmless parasites, but they can be responsible for acne and other skin conditions when they proliferate. As they conceal themselves within the surface of the skin they are difficult to remove by washing. However, the application of antibiotic topical ointments, such as tea tree oil, are very effective at killing the mites and the associated bacteria.

Another mite nearly always present in peoples' homes is the house dust mite *Dermatophagoides pteronyssinus*, which is white in colour. Although it doesn't actually live on the human body, it feeds on the microscopic flakes of skin dander that we shed from our bodies during everyday life and which settle on our floors and beds. Many people have an allergic reaction to house dust due to the presence of dust mite excreta and find themselves violently sneezing and wheezing rhinitis when they inhale the disturbed dust. The best solution is to douse one's face in cold water and rinse one's nostrils to remove the dust. A similar mite *Acarus siro* is known as the grain or flour mite, as it feeds on dry cereals and flour. Infestations contaminate the food with bacteria and excreta, which can result in allergic reactions, diarrhoea and dysentery when the foodstuff is ingested. The mites can also bite, which introduces pathogens into the skin and causes a reaction known as bakers' itch.

Bean Ticks are sometimes found on adults and children when they have been in contact with grass stems, where the ticks sit in wait for a host to brush past. The ticks more usually suck the blood of wild and domestic animals, as they prefer to be hidden within their fur, but they will settle for a human host and find their way to somewhere discreet, such as the groin or an armpit.

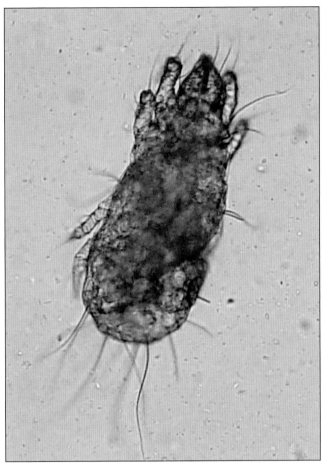

Flour Mite: The flour mite is very similar to the dust mite, but it is vegetarian. *Acarus siro.*

Ticks exploit several hosts as they grow, and the last stage sees them swell with blood to look similar to a castor bean.

The species *Ixodes ricinus*, sometimes known as the deer tick, is particularly common in parts of Britain and is known as a vector for the bacterium *Borrelia burgdorferi*, responsible for Lyme disease, which can have a very debilitating effect on humans. It is always a good idea to remove ticks quickly for this reason, but they can be tricky to loosen from the skin without leaving the mouthparts *in situ*, which often results in an itchy swelling and infection. The most effective method is to hold the tick's head with fine tweezers and gently pull until it releases its grip. Application of petroleum jelly also has the effect of making the tick decide to abandon its host. The bite should then be sterilized with alcohol, iodine tincture or tea-tree oil. If Lyme disease is suspected, then specialist courses of antibiotics should be sought from a doctor. It often begins with a distinctive red ring around the bite, rather like a roundel pattern.

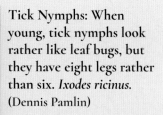

Tick Nymphs: When young, tick nymphs look rather like leaf bugs, but they have eight legs rather than six. *Ixodes ricinus.* (Dennis Pamlin)

Tick unfed: As a tick becomes adult it has a round plate over the abdomen known as the scutum or dorsal shield. *Ixodes ricinus.* (Michel Bernard)

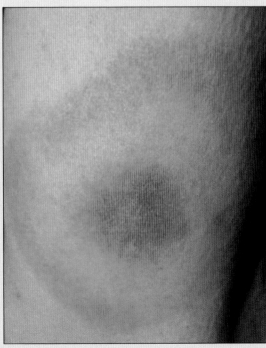

Above: Tick fed: When gorged with blood the tick's abdomen swells like a balloon from beneath the scutum. *Ixodes ricinus.* (Jimmy Rehak)

Lyme Disease: Lyme disease often begins as a red ring that radiates away from the tick bite swelling. *Borrelia burgdorferi.* (F. Butters)

HOUSE CENTIPEDES

The house centipede *Scutigera coleoptrata* originates from the Mediterranean region and therefore relies on human habitations in order to remain warm enough during the winter months in Britain. It is a fearsome looking animal and has a surprisingly rapid running speed. As it is reminiscent of a large spider in appearance and motion, many people have an innate fear of the creature for similar reasons. They appear larger than they really are due to the length of their legs.

In fact, the house centipede can inflict an unpleasant sting with its front legs, which have evolved into fang-like appendages called forcipules. The sting is similar to that of a wasp sting, causing acute pain and localized reddening of the skin. However, house centipedes only bite when trapped or threatened, as they would rather use their venom for securing prey.

They attack and feed on a wide variety of other arthropods, including many pest insect and arachnid species, so they can be considered useful in the home and therefore tolerated rather than eradicated. They are most often encountered when surprised by an electric light being turned on, so they scurry away to find darkness. They are just as startled as the humans.

House centipedes are currently confined to southern Britain, but their range is likely to spread north with global warming. Their favoured habitat is warm and damp cellars, where they can hunt and reproduce. In the wild they live in caves with similar conditions.

House Centipede: The house centipede's head is to the right, but it looks like the tail, so that it fools predators. *Scutigera coleoptrata*. (Alan Couch)

HUMAN LICE

The phrase 'feeling lousy' originates from infestations of lice. There are three kinds that infest humans: the pubic louse, or crab louse – *Pthirus pubis*; the head louse – *Pediculus humanus capitis*; and the body Louse – *Pediculus humanus humanus*. They are most often transferred from one person to another by physical contact. Many people associate them with uncleanliness, but it is really the intimate conditions that often accompany uncleanliness that allow the lice to spread. In fact, lice prefer clean bodies as it is easier for them to bite the skin and suck blood. The head louse and body louse both have elongated bodies like typical insects, while the public louse has a rounded crab-like body. Louse infestations cause irritation and itching. They can transmit diseases, but very rarely. Their lifecycle occurs in three stages. Their eggs are called nits and are glued to hairs in the case of public and head lice or to clothing in the case of body lice. The eggs hatch into nymphs, which then grow into the adult form. Interestingly, the body louse evolved away from the head louse with the advent of human clothing, which occurred about a hundred thousand years ago.

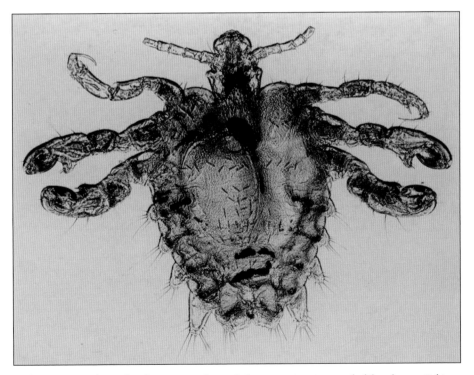

Pubic Louse: The pubic louse is wide and short, giving it a crab-like shape. *Pthirus pubis.* (NMH)

Head Louse: The head louse has hooked claws for holding onto the shafts of hairs. *Pediculus humanus capitis.* (Giles San Martin)

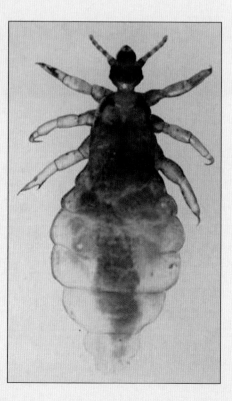

Body Louse: The body louse is larger than the head louse, with longer legs. *Pediculus humanus humanus.* (NMH)

BOOKLICE

The booklice, or paper lice are not related to the human lice. They are wingless species of a group of flying insects known as bark lice or Psocopterans. They are sometimes referred to as the bookworm, but curiously their larvae are nymphs rather than grubs. The larvae actually feed on the mould that grows on old books rather than the paper itself, so that holes gradually appear as the mould progresses. Camphor and other chemicals are used to control booklice, although the best method is to keep the documents in totally dry conditions, so that the mould cannot grow. Booklice will also infest stuffed animals and insect specimens in cabinets. Some species of booklice are more usually found living in cereals and in flour. They can reproduce without mating, just like aphids, enabling them to multiply rapidly when conditions are favourable. Genera of booklice include *Trogium* and *Liposcelis*.

Book Louse: The booklouse is a minute insect that can infest old books in mildly damp conditions, where is feeds on mould and adhesives. *Trogium pulsatorium.* (Andy Murray)

BEDBUGS

The bedbug *Cimex lectularius*, has become more widespread in Britain since the invention of central heating and double glazing. This is because it originates from warmer climates and often hitches a ride in the clothing of unsuspecting holidaymakers and other airborne travellers. As their name suggests, these bugs tend to hide in mattresses and bedding, where they have easy access to human hosts, whose blood they suck. They are not considered to be vectors of disease, but an infestation of bedbugs can result in numerous unpleasant bites, which can lead to secondary infections when they are scratched.

As it is difficult to use chemicals to penetrate mattresses effectively enough, it has been found that other methods or eradication are more useful, such as vacuuming and steaming. Wrapping mattresses with barriers and using open frame beds is also good practice. Bedding should also be left to soak in hot water before washing, in order to drown the eggs, nymphs and adults. Bedbugs are members of the true bug order Hemiptera, but they have lost their wings. They detect the presence of humans by sensing their warmth and the carbon dioxide in their exhaled breath.

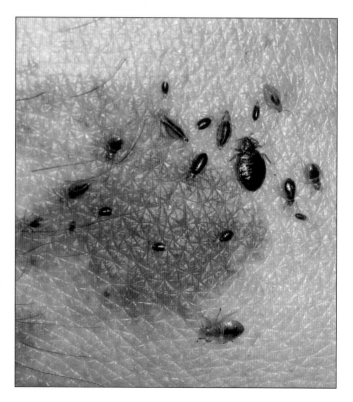

Bugs and Lice: Here both bed bugs and body lice can be seen feeding together. *Cimex lectularius*. *Pediculus humanus humanus.* (Lou Ento)

Bed Bug: An adult bedbug feeding on the blood of a human host. *Cimex lectularius.*

COCKROACHES

Cockroaches are unusual insects, as they are semi-social and they are omnivorous, making them very good at exploiting the resources available to them in human homes and other buildings. Fossil evidence shows that cockroaches have changed little over hundreds of millions of years, because they are so well designed for their lifestyle. They have also seen many other animal clades come and go over that time, which is why cockroaches have a reputation for resilience. Indeed, they are likely to remain unchanged long after humanity has been the author of its own demise due to overpopulation, famine and bellicosity.

There are four species of cockroach associated with humans in Britain. All originate from warmer climes but survive very well alongside humanity due to artificial heating. There are two relatively small species – the German cockroach *Blattella germanica*, and the brown-banded cockroach *Supella longipalpa*. There are two relatively large species – the American, *Periplaneta americana*, and the Oriental, *Blatta orientalis*.

Being semi-social brings certain advantages. For one thing, it means that many cockroaches can hide communally in larger numbers. It also means that located food sources can benefit the cockroach community as a whole. In addition, predators find it far more difficult to prey on animals that travel

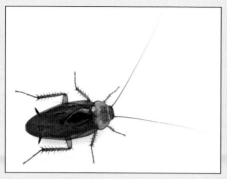

(a)

(b)

(c)

(d)

(e)

(a) American Cockroach (D. Sikes);
(b) German Cockroach (L.M. Buga);
(c) Brown-banded Cockroach
(Non Rev); (d) Oriental Cockroach, male
(K. Schneider) & (e) female (R. Plenty).
Although cockroaches come in a variety
of shapes and sizes, they all have rather
flattened bodies with running legs
and long antennae for sensing their
environment in darkness. *Periplaneta
Americana, Blattella germanica, Supella
longipalpa, Blatta orientalis x 2.*

in groups and randomly scatter when they sense danger. Similarly, being omnivorous means that cockroaches can take advantage of a wide variety of food sources.

In fact, they will eat a surprising range of substances in addition to those that humans think of as food, including soap, paper, human skin, greasy fingerprints, leather, hair, wallpaper paste and sewage. Some of these can only be eaten because certain bacteria break them down chemically, enabling the cockroaches to absorb their nutrients. In the wild, cockroaches feed on the detritus on cave and forest floors, so they have evolved to make the most of materials that other animals do not consider food.

Cockroaches don't spread disease directly, but their presence tends to indicate unhygienic conditions that harbour germs. Therefore, eradication is best achieved by improving hygiene and by removing places where the insects can secrete themselves. If they have nowhere to live, to feed and to breed then they cannot establish colonies.

TERMITES

The Mediterranean termite species *Reticulitermes grassei* has colonized small areas in Southwest England and concerted efforts have been made to eradicate them. This is because termite colonies feed on deadwood, so they are capable of destroying the structural integrity of buildings. The species already exists in latitudes farther north than Britain, such as Canada, so it is really only a matter of time before termites become uncontrollably established. Central heating and global warming already provide congenial conditions and there are many ways in which termites can stow away to our shores from other countries: in timber; in plant pots; in food cargoes; in luggage, and so on.

Termites are quite closely related to cockroaches, and there are some species that fall between the two. Termites have bacteria in their gut that digest the cellulose in wood, thereby enabling the termites to absorb nutrients. Their presence isn't usually obvious as they eat timbers from the inside out, so infestations are often detected too late to save buildings from ruin; i.e. when they begin to collapse.

Eradication of termites is not easy, as sub-colonies can lie deep in the ground and out of reach. In addition, workers can become reproductive when isolated, so new colonies can arise from remnant populations without needing to mate. As they know that any wood supply is finite, they naturally explore their environs in search of new places to set up camp. This is why there has been an effort to prevent termites from becoming established in the first place.

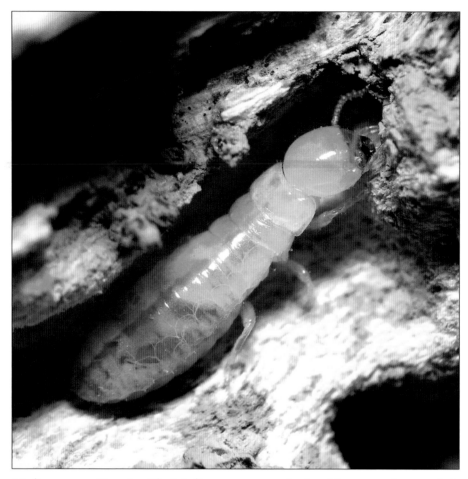

Mediterranean Termite: The Mediterranean termite is seldom seen, because it is usually hidden away inside timber. *Reticulitermes grassei.* (Katja Schulz)

FLEAS

Fleas have a long association with human habitations. Adult fleas feed on the blood of host mammals, including people, and the larvae feed on detritus, including skin flakes found in house dust. The human flea, or house flea, is *Pulex irritans*. Despite its name, it will also feed on the blood of other mammals, both domestic and wild, which enables it to travel from one habitation to another. Domestic cats and dogs have their own flea species too: *Ctenocephalides felis* and *Ctenocephalides canis*. Both will also feed on humans when they find themselves without a host.

In fact, there are many species of flea that find themselves in houses because they are brought in by dogs and cats that pick them up from small mammals

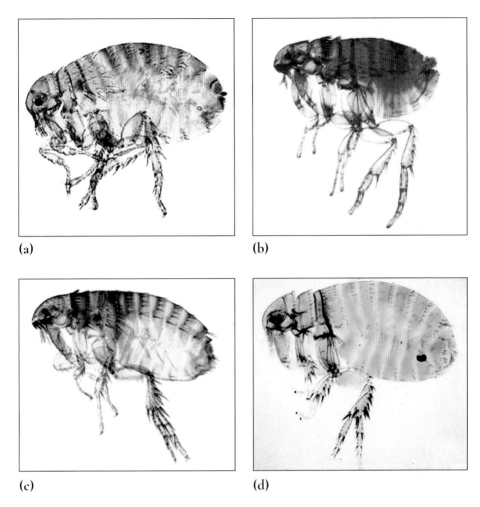

(a)

(b)

(c)

(d)

(a) Human Flea; (b) Cat Flea; (c) Dog Flea; (d) Rat Flea: All domestic fleas are rather similar in appearance, as they have evolved with very similar lifestyles even though they tend to prefer particular host species. (Michael Wunderli)

in gardens, parks and so on. This is why fleas vary so much in size and colour, from tiny and black to easily visible and brown. Flea bodies are very narrow, so that they can move rapidly between the hairs of their hosts. They have no wings, but instead have the ability to jump very quickly and over considerable distances in order to reach the bodies of passing hosts.

Of course, fleas cause extreme irritation with their bites, which can also become infected when the skin is scratched raw. Worse than this, fleas can also spread contagious diseases, so it is always wise to eradicate them. The best method is to use sprays that kill eggs, larvae and adults, and to frequently and thoroughly vacuum carpets, soft furnishings and bedding to remove detritus.

There are also chemicals that can be applied to cats and dogs to make them distasteful to fleas.

Other genera of small mammal flea include *Xenopsylla, Amalaraeus, Ctenophthalmus, Doratopsylla, Hystrichopsylla, Megabothris, Peromyscopsylla, Rhadinopsylla,* They are all rather similar and usually require investigation under a microscope to identify. They are found on rodents, moles, hedgehogs, shrews, squirrels and so on.

BEETLES

The reason why beetles are found in human homes is that their larvae feed on a variety of materials and substances found in them. Some species have larvae that feed on dead wood and paper, while others feed on leather, wool and dried cereals, flour and other substances.

The larva of the common furniture beetle *Anobium punctatum* is responsible for the holes in wooden furniture that we call woodworm. The larva looks like a small white grub or worm. A medium sized species is *Xestobium rufovillosum*, often known as the deathwatch beetle, due to a tapping noise once thought to be an omen of death. Occasionally a larger species is found, known as the house longhorn beetles, *Hylotrupes bajulus*. All three leave tunnels in wood used to make furniture and house structures. The tunnels radiate from the point where the eggs are laid, and they become progressively wider as the larvae grow. They pupate close to the surface of the wood, so that the adults can easily emerge when they hatch out.

Beetles with larvae that feed on other substances around the home include the specimen beetle, *Anthrenus museorum*; the variegated carpet beetle, *Anthrenus varbasci*; the spotted carpet or fur beetles, *Attagenus pellio*; the flour beetle,

Woodworm Beetle: The woodworm beetle is very small and often goes unnoticed until the damage is done. *Anobium punctatum.* (Kentish Plumber)

Woodworm Larva: The woodworm larva has vestigial legs, as it is a grub rather than a worm. *Anobium punctatum.*

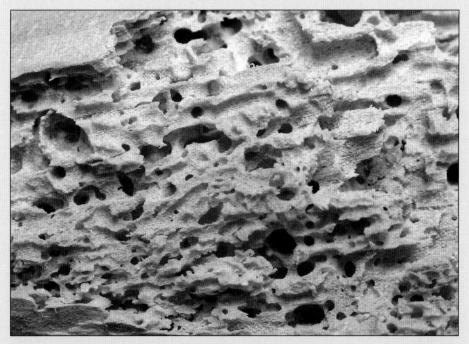

Woodworm Damage: An infestation of woodworm causes timber to completely disintegrate.

Deathwatch Beetle: The deathwatch beetle communicates by making a tapping noise with its thorax. *Xestobium rufovillosum*. (Giles San Martin)

Deathwatch Damage: The tunnels of the deathwatch larvae grow as the grubs increase in girth. *Xestobium rufovillosum*. (Martin Fisch)

Longhorn Beetle: The longhorn beetle actually has long antennae rather than horns. *Hylotrupes bajulus.*

Longhorn Larva: The longhorn larva has tough mouthparts for chewing wood fibres. *Hylotrupes bajulus.*

Specimen Beetle: The larvae of the specimen beetle will feed on the desiccated or mummified remains of animals, such as stuffed mammals and birds, or pinned insects. *Anthrenus museorum.* (Joni Rasanen)

(a)

(b)

(a) Variegated Carpet Beetle (Larah McElroy); (b) Spotted Carpet Beetle; (c) Carpet Beetle Larva: The larvae of the variegated and spotted carpet beetle feed on fur and woollen fibres, which are often found in carpets. *Anthrenus varbasci, Attagenus pellio.* (Nikon Ranger)

(c)

Tribolium destructor; the yellow mealworm beetle, *Tenebrio molitor*; the larder beetle, *Dermestes lardarius*; the tobacco beetle, *Lasioderma serricorne*; and the biscuit weevil, *Stegobium paniceum*. The adults of all these beetles can fly, so they have no problem finding mates and finding food for their larvae. Their larvae are adapted to feeding on foods with low levels of moisture, as they tend to pupate within the same substances as protection from predators.

(a)

(b)

(c)

(d)

(e)

(a) Flour Beetle; (b) Yellow Mealworm Beetle; (c) Larder Beetle (Gail Hampshire); (d) Tobacco Beetle (G. Bohne); (e) Biscuit Weevil: The larvae of the flour beetle, yellow Mealworm beetle, the larder beetle, the tobacco beetle and the biscuit weevil will eat just about any dried foodstuff or commodity kept in the kitchen or pantry. (Christophe Quintin)

MOTHS

A number of small moths do very well living in our homes. The common or webbing clothes moth, *Tineola bisselliella*; the case-bearing clothes moth, *Tinea pellionella*; the white-shouldered house moth, *Endrosis sarcitrella*; the brown house moth, *Hofmannophila pseudospretella*; and the carpet or tapestry moth, *Trichophaga tapetzella* all have caterpillars that feed on natural fibres, such as wool, cotton, linen, silk, feathers, fur and hair, which are found in clothes, furnishings and carpets. Their presence often goes unnoticed until the adults begin flying about rooms in search of mates and places to lay their eggs. It then becomes apparent that household items have become perforated by the caterpillars. Often the cocoons are also visible on the surface.

(a)

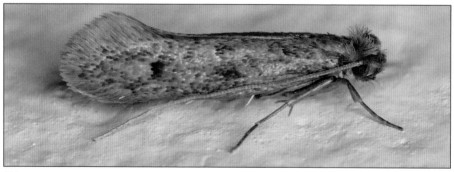

(b)

(a) **Common Clothes Moth** (Vlad Peoklov); (b) **Case-bearing Clothes Moth:** The common clothes moth and the white-shouldered house moth will infest clothing and textiles made from natural fibres. *Tineola bisselliella, Tinea pellionella.* (Patrick Clement)

(a) **White-shouldered House Moth** (Gail Hampshire); (b) **Brown House** (Patrick Clement); (c) **Tapestry Moth**: The white-shouldered house moth, brown house moth and tapestry moth will infest furniture fabrics, carpets and curtains made from natural fibres. *Endrosis sarcitrella, Hofmannophila pseudospretella. Trichophaga tapetzella.* (R. Sheeger)

(a)

(b)

(c)

(a)

(b)

(a) Codling Moth (Ben Sale); (b) Codling Moth Caterpillar: The caterpillar of the codling moth is often known as a worm or maggot due to its white and smooth skin. *Cydia pomonella.* (Giles San Martin)

Occasionally, codling moths, *Cydia pomonella*, are seen flying in houses too, having hatched from apples, as they are responsible for the apple 'maggot' which is really a caterpillar. Similarly, the Indian meal moth, *Plodia interpunctella*, is occasionally found in kitchens, where its larvae feed on dried cereals and flour. The Mediterranean flour moth, *Ephestia kuehniella*, is a pest of the same foodstuffs. Both species have become established in Britain due to central heating and global warming.

(a)

(b)

(a) Indian Meal Moth (Don Hobern); (b) Mediterranean Four Moth: The larvae of Indian meal moth and the Mediterranean flour moth both feed on the meal or flour ground from wheat, oats, and other cereals. (A. Reago & C.M. McClarren)

HOUSE CRICKET

The house cricket, *Acheta domesticus*, was introduced to Britain via pet shops, which sell the insects as live food for reptiles. It has become established due to central heating and global warming, which enable it to survive the winter. There are also populations at landfill sites due to the warmth of decomposition and the available food, In houses, these crickets cause no particular harm, but they are a nuisance because they incessantly chirp to communicate with one another, day and night. That said, some people enjoy their song and still others enjoy eating them, rather like terrestrial prawns. The house cricket is a species of true cricket, or ground cricket, with an omnivorous diet.

House Cricket:
The house cricket looks similar to a cockroach, but its body is not flattened. *Acheta domesticus.*
(K. Schneider)

WASPS

In the wild, the common wasp, *Vespula vulgaris*, builds its nest in caves, cavities within trees or in abandoned rabbit holes., because they are dark and dry. This means that loft spaces are very attractive as nesting sites. In addition,

(K.P. Bur)

(Pver Donk)

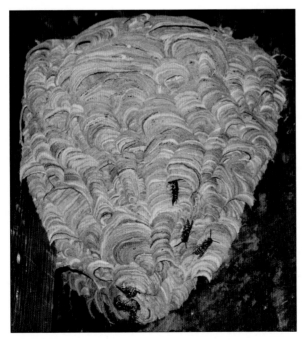

Common Wasp & Nest: The nest of the common wasp will keep growing through the year as long as there is space. *Vespula vulgaris.*

(Derek Parker)

Hornet & Nest:
The hornet is far
larger than the
common wasp and
it has a more fulvous
coloration. *Vespa
crabro*.

(M. Kucharczyk)

wasps make papier-mâché from dead wood to build their nests, so the roof
beams are ideal places to collect the raw material they need. As their nests
can grow to house many thousands of insects, then they pose a genuine threat
to people when they sense a threat to their larvae. They will attack and sting
en masse, so it is always wise to eradicate them. Our largest wasp, the hornet,
Vespa crabro, will occasionally nest in houses too, but it is less aggressive even
though its size and noise can feel intimidating.

BEES

The tree bumblebee, *Bombus hypnorum* will occasionally nest in the eaves of houses. Bumblebees build relatively small nests from wax and they are seldom aggressive, so they don't present a problem. People sometimes mistake them for honeybees, *Apis mellifera*, as the worker bumblebees are quite small and dark in colour. Upon closer inspection, they are actually black and hairy, with a reddish tail-end. Honeybees are far less hairy and brownish in colour.

(Gail Hampshire)

Tree Bumblebee & Nest: The tree bumblebee repurposes old bird nests which it finds in beneath the eaves of houses. *Bombus hypnorum.*

(O. Aurochs)

(P. Delia)

Honey Bee & Nest: The natural nest of the honey bee comprises hanging waxen curtains filled with hexagonal breed and storage cells. *Apis mellifera.*

Honeybees do occasionally nest in roof spaces too and can build enormous nests. Wasp and bumblebee nests are abandoned in the autumn, but honeybee nests remain active all year, as the honey provides food during the winter months. So, honeybee nests continue to grow year on year. Like wasps, honeybees can become very aggressive in defence of their nests. Worse than wasps, they leave their stingers in one's flesh.

There is an urban myth that bee and wasp stings can be neutralized by the application of baking soda and malt vinegar, as the stings are acidic and alkaline, respectively. Although this idea is based on scientific logic, the stings contain many other substances that cause the pain and cannot be neutralized, It seems that people experience a placebo effect due to their belief and the cooling effect of applying the liquids. The only effective remedy is to keep the sting cool with water or ice and to wait for the body to remove the venom naturally. Some people suffer anaphylactic reactions to stings, so antihistamines are necessary to prevent serious complications from the toxins. Of course, the best strategy is to minimize the risk of being stung in the first place.

ANTS

The reason why ants are drawn to kitchens is the lure of sugars in particular. In the wild sugars can be found in flower nectar, fruits and the honeydew of aphids, but these are in relatively short supply. So, when ants find sugar in the form of crystals or candy they get very enthusiastic. The pioneering worker ant will soon return to the nest with her good news, having left a trail of pheromones, so that her fellow workers can find their way to the prize. As a result, people often find ant trails in their kitchens, leading to and from the supply of sugar or sugary food, such as cakes and biscuits.

The most common culprit is the black ant, *Lasius niger*, as it has a tendency to wander considerable distances from the nest. It is also a small ant, enabling it to gain access through the tiniest of holes. The common red ant, *Myrmica rubra*, will also come into kitchens in search of easy food. A third common species is the meadow ant, *Lasius flavus*. If ants prove troublesome then the best way to deal with the problem is to block their point of access and remove the temptation. Of course, one might also leave morsels of food near to the point of entry, so they have no need to travel through the kitchen.

Black Ant: The black ant is the most frequent house invader in England, where it searches for sugary fluids in particular. *Lasisu niger*. (Didier 85)

Red Ant: The red ant is larger and slower moving than the Lasius ants and is also able to sting. *Myrmica rubra.*

Meadow Ant: The meadow ant is very similar to the black ant, but it is always yellowish in colour. *Lasius flavus.*

WOODLICE

The common smooth woodlouse, *Oniscus asellus*, and the common rough woodlouse, *Porcello scaber*, can often be found in older houses, particularly behind the skirting boards, where they feeds on decaying wood. Woodlice, or slaters, also have the curious habit of wandering into electrical sockets and light fitting along the wires, where they then grow too large to escape.

(a)

(b)

(a) Smooth Woodlouse (B. Wrangler); (b) Rough Woodlouse: The smooth woodlouse and the rough woodlouse grow as nymphs, so they are able to find their way through very small gaps and then become trapped as they grow. *Oniscus asellus, Porcello scaber.* (K. Schulz)

Often many hundreds of dead woodlice can be found when these fittings are opened. Woodlice don't pose a problem in themselves, but they are an indicator of dampness in a property, so they should be seen as a signal that remedial work may be required to prevent timber rot.

SILVERFISH

The common silverfish, *Lepisma saccharina*, is a wingless primitive insect-like arthropod – a hexapod – that has a silvery colour and a fish-like body covered with scales. It is often found in pantries and larders, where it feeds

(a)

(b)

(c)

(a) Silverfish (Eran Finkle);
(b) Bristletail (Andy Murray);
(c) Springtail: The silverfish, springtail and bristletail are all primitive insect-like animals known as hexapods. *Lepisma saccharina, Tomocerus vulgaris, Campodea fragilis.* (Christophe Quintin)

on sugary and starchy foods that have been spilled. It will also eat the starch from adhesives, used in books, furniture and carpets. Anything that contains some form of carbohydrate is considered food, including fats. People usually notice them when the insects are caught in the open as a light is switched, or when they move something under which silverfish happen to be hiding. They are not particularly problematic, but large numbers of silverfish can be unhygienic and cause damage to food and possessions.

Two other types of hexapod can be found in houses too: the springtail and the two-pronged bristletail. Examples are the common springtail, *Tomocerus vulgaris* and the white bristletail, *Campodea fragilis*. They feed on moulds and detritus in damp places.

PARASITIC WORMS

If the idea of parasites on the outside of the body is disagreeable, then the idea of parasites inside the body is truly unpleasant. The most frequent parasitic worm in Britain is *Enterobius vermicularis*, variously known as threadworm, pinworm or simply 'worms'. Many children get threadworm, which causes an itchy bottom due to the activity of the worms at night, as they exit the anus to lay their eggs and then return to the bowel. In this way, children scratch their bottoms and pick up the eggs on their fingers, which are then transferred to the mouth or to new hosts. Threadworm is quite easily dealt with by ingesting chemical pills and washing bedding.

Less common in humans, but potentially more serious are *Ascaris lumbricoides*, the roundworm, and *Dipylidium caninum* and *Echinococcus*

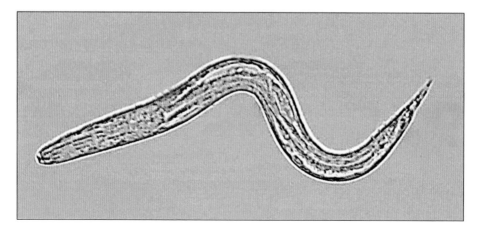

Threadworm: The threadworm is a very small parasitic intestinal worm commonly found in children. *Enterobius vermicularis.* (R. Sheeger)

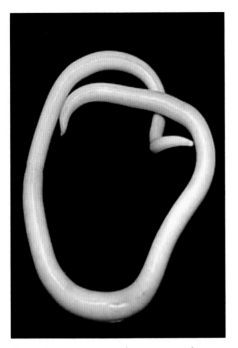

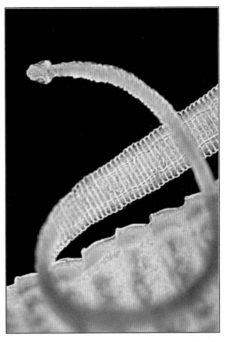

Roundworm: Roundworms are large parasitic intestinal worms that look rather like smooth earthworms. *Ascaris lumbricoides.* (R. Sheeger)

Tapeworm: Tapeworms are intestinal parasitic worms that have segments, which break away and generate into new worms. *Dipylidium caninum, Echinococcus granulosus.* (Justin)

granulosus which are tapeworms, otherwise known as Cestodes worms. The roundworm is a nematode with a pernicious lifecycle that involves a larval stage within body organs and an adult stage within the gut, so treatment is essential.

The *Dipylidium caninum* tapeworm is more usually found in domestic dogs and cats, but it can transfer to children by ingestion. The worm itself breaks into small sections which can be seen crawling around the anus of pet animals. Infestations can be debilitating in humans, as the worms steal nutrients from the body. The *Echinococcus granulosus* tapeworm causes cysts to grow within the body, which are dangerous and difficult to treat. For these reasons, hygiene regarding pet animals and livestock should always be maintained, as it is better to avoid contracting parasitic worms of any kind than to have to seek medical attention. This, of course, involves the education of both children and adults, so that they understand the risks and behave appropriately.

(a) Tender Slug;
(b) Field Slug
(Christophe Quintin);
(c) Cellar Slug: The yellow slug, tender slug, field slug and cellar slug are all similarly sized slugs that enter our homes at night and then hide in damp dark places during the day. *Malacolimax tenellus, Deroceras reticulatum, Limacus maculatus.* (S. Brainfield)

(a)

(b)

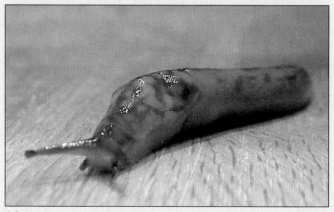

(c)

SLUGS

Slugs are closely related to snails, but having no shell enables them to squeeze though tight gaps, around doors and windows. They often come into kitchens, attracted by pet food and bins, and the smooth floors of kitchen suit their way of moving. Once inside a kitchen, they will then seek places to hide during the day, underneath fridges and dishwashers, so that the food supply is easy to reach at night. Various common species of slug can become indoor pests in this way, as slugs are often omnivorous, and will eat a wide variety of substances. Often, they lick surfaces with traces of food that are not evident to people, and this is often the trail they follow into a kitchen in the first place. The best way to deal with kitchen slugs is to remove them and then be more fastidious about keeping one's kitchen clean, so that they are not enticed by the lure of food. As it is not easy to block their points of entry, then it can be easier to use a chemical barrier of some kind, such as a film of repellent, on the floor or the door frame. The species that tend to enter our homes are small to medium in size, as they can squeeze through the narrowest gaps.

FLIES

There are many species of fly that inhabit houses, either because their larvae feed on something within houses or because the adult flies do; sometimes both. To many people, flies are a real nuisance simply because they pester and irritate, but flies can also spread germs and bite, so many ways have been devised to kill or deter them – fly papers, UV traps, bait traps, fly screens, fly sprays, and so on.

The most obvious fly species to discuss first are the housefly, *Musca domestica*, and the lesser House Fly, *Fannia canicularis*. Both species are very commonly found in association with humans. Their larvae feed on all manner of decaying foods, including meat and faeces, so the flies are responsible for the spread of germs. The lesser housefly will also lay its eggs in lesions on people's skin, so that the larvae burrow beneath the skin, causing boils and infection – myiasis. House flies tend to fly about rooms and frequently land, as they taste for potential foods with their feet. Lesser houseflies are smaller and have the habit of flying around in circles below light fittings. Although the two species are similar in appearance and habits, they actually belong to different fly families.

There is a species of fly very similar to the housefly called the stable fly, *Stomoxys calcitrans*, which is a biting fly. Instead of a sucking proboscis, the

Housefly: The housefly is a medium sized fly found in and around human homes in urban, suburban and rural places. *Musca domestica.* (S. Rae)

Lesser Housefly: The lesser housefly is smaller than the housefly and has a relatively skinny abdomen. *Fannia canicularis.* (Janet Graham)

Stable Fly: The stable fly is similar in size and appearance to the housefly, but it has a piercing proboscis. *Stomoxys calcitrans.* (Bernard Ruelle)

stable fly has piercing proboscis for taking the blood of mammals, including humans. Its larvae feed on the dung of livestock, so the flies are more common in rural areas. Like the housefly, the stable fly enters houses, but it is more annoying as it frequently lands on people in search of a blood meal. The bite is felt as a sharp pricking sensation. In Britain the stable fly is an irritation, but elsewhere in the world it is a vector of disease.

Blowflies are larger flies with larvae that feed on carrion, which includes raw meats, cured meats, cooked meats and fish. They will readily lay their eggs on these foodstuffs given half a chance, so they can be real nuisances in the summer months if food is left out on tables and surfaces. They have even been known to enter cupboards and refrigerators to reach suitable food for their larvae. The adult flies will also feed on the fluids of faeces, so they spread bacteria onto human food with their feet and mouthparts. Common blowfly species include the blackbottle, *Calliphora livida*, the bluebottle, *Calliphora vomitoria*, the greenbottles, *Lucilia sericata*, and the flesh fly, *Sarcophaga bercaea*.

A species of fly in the same family as the blowflies is the cluster fly, *Pollenia rudis*, so called because it has the habit of hibernating by clustering together in attics and roof spaces. They don't cause any damage, but they can congregate in enormous numbers, which entices other creatures to arrive. Cluster fly larvae feed only on earthworms. The adult flies have a cosmopolitan diet of decaying animal and vegetable matter.

(a) Blackbottle (Gail Hampshire); (b) Bluebottle (S. Sputzer); (c) Greenbottle: The blackbottle, bluebottle and greenbottle are all large glossy flies attracted to carrion and faeces. *Calliphora livida, Calliphora vomitoria, Lucilia sericata.* (Ls Nikk)

Flesh Fly: The flesh fly is a large fly with characteristically pads on its feet and striped thorax. *Sarcophaga bercaea.* (Janet Graham)

Cluster Fly: The cluster fly has a golden downy thorax and is rather slow moving compared with other flies. *Pollenia rudis.* (Martin Cooper)

(a) Common Horsefly (Janet Graham); (b) Brown Horsefly (Gail Hampshire);
(c) Giant Horsefly: Female common horseflies, brown horseflies and giant horseflies
all inject an anaesthetic when they bite, which subsequently causes severe itchiness.
Haematopota pluvialis, Tabanus bromius, Tabanus seduticus. (Frank Vassen)

Horseflies, sometimes known as gadflies and clegs, are far more intimidating than stable flies, due to their size, and their bites are far more irritating because they develop into very itchy hives. This is because horseflies inject an anaesthetic so that the host animal doesn't feel the bite. The foreign chemicals then cause a reaction as the body begins to remove them. Horseflies come in a variety of sizes, from medium sized flies to very large flies, so their bite would be very noticeable without the anaesthetic. They sense the sweat of their hosts and then home in, so they will enter houses in search of human hosts on hot days. They will pursue their hosts, which is very annoying. Only the females drink blood, as they need the nutrition to develop their eggs. The larvae feed on decaying vegetable matter. Horsefly species include *Haematopota pluvialis*, *Tabanus bromius* and *Tabanus seduticus*. Like the stable fly, they all have the potential for spreading disease.

Other groups of biting flies include the house mosquitoes – Culicidae. They have larvae that live in water, so nearby ponds, water butts and streams often contain the larvae of one species or another. The females require blood to develop their eggs and will often enter houses in search of human hosts, which they detect by warmth and odour. The larger species are often seen

Common House Mosquito: The common house mosquito has a characteristic way of perching on just four legs, but its hind legs are used to sit on water to lay its eggs. *Culex pipiens.* (Gail Hampshire)

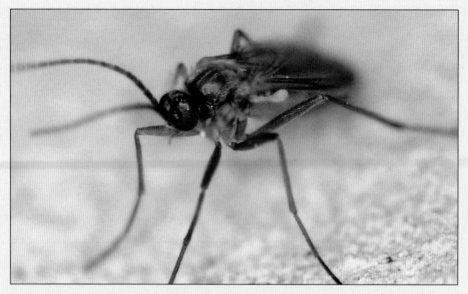

Fungus Gnat: Fungus gnats are most common where people overwater plants, so that decay and fungal growth occurs. *Bradysia polonica.* (Andy Murray)

Crane Fly: Crane flies resemble giant mosquitoes, but they don't feed at all as adults. *Tipula maxima.* (Gail Hampshire)

Drain Fly: The drain fly looks rather like a micro-moth due to the hairiness of its wings. *Berdeniella sp.* (Janet Graham)

perched on walls during the day. The smaller species can go unnoticed until the night time, when their high-pitched noise betrays their presence as they fly past one's ear.

A similar looking group of flies are known as fungus gnats, Sciaridae. Their larvae feed on moulds that grow in the pots of house plants, so they are very common in houses, but the adult flies don't bite. Crane flies, Tipulidae, look like giant mosquitoes and often come into house at night when attracted by lights. They don't even have working mouthparts, as their sole purpose in life is to reproduce. A third group of flies are known as drain gnats, Psychodidae. Their larvae feed on detritus in drains and the adults look like miniature moths, as their wings are opaque. They don't bite either.

A very common and very small fly common in houses is the fruit fly – *Drosophila melanogaster*. It is attracted by the odour given off by fruit, fruit juice and even wine and vinegar, because it lays its eggs on perished fruit flesh. The fruit fly is famous as a laboratory species for experimenting with

Fruit Fly: The fruit fly, or vinegar fly, is attracted by the aromas emitted by decaying and fermenting fruit. *Drosophila sp.* (K. Schulz)

biological inheritance, because it reproduces several times over a single year – it is multivoltine – and it has traits that have simple genetic coding. Fruit flies do no harm in houses, although infestations can be annoying as they will drown in a glass of wine and get stuck in fruit salads.

FLYING BUGS

The term 'bug' is accurately used to describe a particular order of insects – Hemiptera – rather than being used as a generic name for invertebrates. Bugs are similar to beetles, but they have soft wing cases and sucking mouthparts. Three types of very small bug, which often go unnoticed until their numbers multiply, are white fly, *Trialeurodes vaporariorum*, aphids, such as the rose greenfly *Macrosiphum rosae*, and the blackfly, *Aphis fabae*, and scale insects, such as the greenhouse mealy bug, *Pseudococcus calceolariae*. Various species will colonise houseplants and greenhouse plants. They are sometimes introduced as stowaways on cut flowers and they do well in the relatively dry and warm environment.

White Fly: The white fly looks rather like a minute white moth, but it is actually a member of the bug order. *Trialeurodes vaporariorum.* (G. Bohne)

Rose Aphid: The rose aphid is also known as the greenfly, but it is often pinkish in colour. *Macrosiphum rosae.* (Cali Gula)

Black Bean Aphid: The black bean aphid has its name due to its blackish colour and its bean-like shape. *Aphis fabae.* (S. Kohlmann)

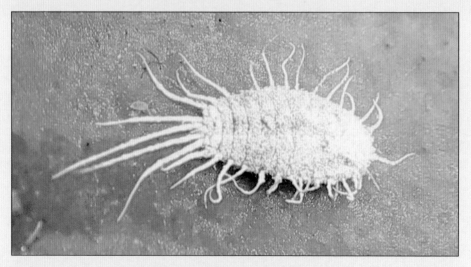

Greenhouse Mealy Bug: The greenhouse mealy bug can become a pest in the warm conditions of glasshouses. *Pseudococcus calceolariae.* (David Short)

BUTTERFLIES AND MOTHS

Quite a number of moth species are attracted to artificial lights at night. It is generally understood that moths will use the moon as a static point in the sky for the purpose of remaining on course when flying in darkness. Therefore, the reason why they fly in circles around lights is that they confuse the light for the moon and attempt to keep it in the same place in their line of vision. Another theory is that they mistake the light for daybreak and get confused

(a)

(b)

(c)

(a) Peacock Butterfly (L. Spindler); (b) Small Tortoiseshell (G. Cheshire); (c) Red Admiral: The peacock, small tortoiseshell and red admiral all have cryptic underwing colouring, to act as camouflage whilst they hibernate. *Aglais io, Aglais urticae, Vanessa atalanta.* (J. Triepke)

because it comes from a single point as they attempt to orientate themselves. Moths will also fly when there is no moon, as they need to get on with the business of reproduction, so it may be that they are more readily lured by artificial lights when the moon is obscured by clouds.

There are also moth and butterfly species that use roof-spaces, sheds and outhouses for the purpose of hibernation. The butterflies that hibernate in houses are the peacock, *Aglais io*, the small tortoiseshell, *Aglais urticae*, and the red admiral, *Vanessa atalanta*. These butterflies all have cryptic underwing markings, so that they are camouflaged in the darkness of tree cavities in the wild. They therefore seek out places that are dark and dry in our homes as substitutes for tree cavities. However, they must also be cold, so that their hibernation is not interrupted. In fact, red admirals are often seen flying on sunny winter days, because the warmth wakes them.

FLORA

lthough the word 'flora' more accurately describes plant-life, as opposed to 'fauna' which describes animals, it is also used to encompass fungi moulds, yeasts, slime moulds, bacteria germs, microbes, biotics, bugs, bacilli and viruses, which are neither plant nor animal, but grow and multiply in a similar way to algae, which are simple plants – often single-celled. These organisms are often invisible to the naked eye, until they multiply in such numbers that their presence becomes evident as a patch of colour.

SIMPLE PLANTS

Most houses have simple plants growing on their roof tiles, on their exterior walls and sometimes inside where conditions are always damp. The most common simple plants are mosses, algae and lichens. Instead of producing seeds, these plants produce spores. They are so small that they become airborne and are therefore able to find their way to new places to grow, so new plants seem to magically appear. Mosses are the most plant-like in structure, as they have the ability to grow green leaflets and branch out. They usually form dome shaped masses, but they will also form carpets over surface areas if conditions are suitable. Algae don't have structure, but grow as a film of cells in damp conditions, so that the surface appears to have a green covering. Lichens are described as symbiotic organisms, as they are half fungus-half alga, or half fungus-half cyanobacterium. They live together, because they are able to provide something that the other lacks, so they both benefit from the arrangement.

Species: mosses, algae, lichens constituents.

SIMPLE FUNGI

The types of simple fungi that colonise damp surfaces and damp timbers in houses are usually described as moulds, slime-moulds and rots. Like the simple plants, these fungi also produce spores. When they are abundant in the air they can cause breathing conditions and illness, because they get into people's noses and lungs. This can lead to asthma, allergic reactions and toxic reactions.

SURFACE MOULDS

There are various types of mould known as black mould: *Stachybotrys chartarum*; *Aspergillus niger*; *Cladosporium herbarum*. These are the moulds found growing in damp corners, on window frames, on the grouting in between tiles and on the sealant in showers. They are usually blackish-green in colour.

FOOD MOULDS

Another place to commonly find moulds, is on stale bread and overripe fruit. *Rhizopus stolonifer* is known as black bread mould, while *Neurospora crassa* is known as red bread mould. Perhaps the most common bread mould is *Penicillium notatum*, which is a pale blue-green colour. Other *Penicillium* species are responsible for the veining in blue cheeses, such as stilton and Roquefort. They are also responsible for the white skin on soft cheeses, such Camembert and brie. The antibiotic penicillin is derived from these moulds, as they have evolved to produce chemicals that are toxic to bacteria, so that they can colonize food sources without competition.

Bread Mould: Various types of mould can be seen growing on this piece of stale bread.

When these moulds grow on fruit they are often alongside the brown fruit mould *Monilinia fructicola*. There is also a mould often found on leaf vegetables, known as leaf blight, *Alternaria alternata*, which causes brown and yellow patches.

Some rots and blights are not caused by fungi, but other types of microscopic organism. There are species of bacteria, in the genus *Pectobacterium*, which feed on the roots, tubers, bulbs, corms and rhizomes of stored vegetables. For example, *Pectobacterium atrosepticum* attacks potatoes, and *Pectobacterium carotovorum* attacks carrots. If they are already present when the vegetables are harvested, then they continue to infest the crop. Similarly, *Phytophthora infestans* is a type of amoeba single-celled animal that causes rot in potatoes and tomatoes.

TIMBER ROTS

When people talk of timber rot, they are generally describing the effect of the mycelium of a fungus as it digests the cellulose structure of the wood, so that it softens and begins to fragment. There are many species of fungus that grow on dead wood in this way. Two common white rot, or soft rot, species are the

Dry Rot: Dry rot causes timber fibres to weaken so that the wood dries and cracks apart across the grain. (Marcus Ward)

Wet Rot: Wet rot causes timber fibres to soften and gradually disintegrate. (R. Sheeger)

cellar fungus *Coniophora puteana* and the spreading fungus *Fibroporia vaillantii*. They both prefer wood that is consistently damp, such as external window frames and doorframes, places where water leaks occur and places where rising damp occurs. A third species, *Serpula lacrymans,* is known as brown rot, or dry rot, because it prefers lower moisture levels and can therefore take hold in timbers that are not visibly wet. White rots turn the wood soft, spongy and fibrous, while brown rot causes the wood to shrink in size and segment into cube-shaped pieces.

PATHOGENIC MOULDS

In addition to the moulds that find places to grow in our homes, there are some moulds that find places to grow on our bodies and have spores that lie about our homes waiting for an opportunity to germinate and grow. They are often described as yeast infections and fungal diseases.

A common pathogenic yeast is *Candida albicans*. It flourishes in naturally moist regions of the body – particularly the genitals and the mouth. It is often known as thrush, because it causes a pattern on the tongue that is reminiscent of the spotted plumage of a thrush bird. People often have sweaty feet too, which provides the ideal environment for *Trichophyton rubrum*, which is responsible for athlete's foot tinea pedis and toenail fungus tinea unguium. Yeasts that prefer drier conditions include *Epidermophyton floccosum*, which causes ring-worm, and *Malassezia globosa*, which causes dandruff. All of these moulds feed on dead skin, sebum and other body detritus, residues and excreta.

ENVIRONMENTAL BACTERIA

Just as the spores of simple plants and fungi sit on surfaces waiting for their opportunity to germinate and grow, so bacteria do much the same. Bacteria don't produce spores, as they are so small that they simply multiply by splitting in two, which is called cytokinesis.

Some bacteria are described as 'friendly' bacteria, because they are part of the natural microflora in our intestines and help us in some way. For example, *Lactobacillus casei* produces enzymes that help us digest carbohydrates, and *Bifidobacterium longum* produces chemicals that fend off pathogenic bacteria. In exchange, they have somewhere to live and feed. In other words, we have a symbiotic relationship with these bacteria, as both parties benefit from the arrangement. They are sometimes called probiotics for this reason.

Most bacteria are pathogenic however, as they are not beneficial and cause infections and illness. Some actually live in our large intestine and bowel, which is why our faeces are germ ridden, but they don't usually cause disease because probiotics keep them in their place within the gut. It is when they enter the mouth, wounds and other places and have the chance to overwhelm our defences that we have problems. These harmful bacteria release chemicals that are toxic, so they make us feel ill by poisoning our bodies and our blood. Our white blood cells are able to defend the body by killing the bacteria and neutralizing their toxins, but it is often necessary to use antibiotics as a way of assisting our natural defences. It makes a great deal of sense therefore, to eliminate surface bacteria by being more fastidious about hygiene, so that bacterial infections are less likely to occur. Disinfectants and antiseptics are used for killing bacteria on surfaces and on our bodies.

In recent years a type of bacterium – *Staphylococcus aureus* – has becomes very well known, because there is a strain known as MRSA methicillin-resistant *Staphylococcus aureus* which is highly resistant to synthetic antibiotics and is therefore quite dangerous to children and the elderly, because it is difficult to treat once an infection has taken hold. Its reputation has earned it the moniker 'super bug' as it has proven difficult to sterilize hospitals where people are most vulnerable to infection following surgery.

The common form of *Staphylococcus aureus* is responsible for skin infections, tooth abscesses, septic cuts and boils. It is among many household bacteria, which can cause a whole list of ailments. For example: *Clostridium* species cause diarrhoea, botulism, cellulitis and tetanus. *Listeria* species cause sepsis, meningitis and weakened immunity. Species of *Salmonella* and *Campylobacter* cause food poisoning. *Propionibacterium acnes* causes acne. *Helicobacter pylori* causes stomach ulcers.

ENVIRONMENTAL VIRUSES

Most viruses require direct transfer from one host organism to another in order to survive, because they need host cells in which to multiply. There are a few though, that can survive for short periods of time on surfaces in appropriate conditions. The Human papilloma virus, which is responsible for verrucae or plantar warts *Verruca plantaris* and common warts *Verruca* vulgaris, can survive in warm fluids for long enough to transmit from one person to another. The *Herpes simplex* virus, responsible for cold sores, whitlows and genital lesions, can similarly be spread by the sharing of eating utensils, lip-balms, drinking vessels and so on. A similar condition, known as herpes zoster, is caused by the chickenpox virus, *Varicella zoster*.